The Hotel Industry:
A High Turnover Industry

by

Fawaz Al-Malood

Copyright

The Hotel Industry: A High Turnover Industry

Copyright © 2023 by Fawaz Al-Malood

To request permission, email the author using the web contact form at: https://dralmalood.com/contact

Published by: Dr. Fawaz Al-Malood, California
Website: https://www.dralmalood.com/

Edited by: Natalie Perdue
Website: https://yarrowediting.com

Cover Design by: Dario from Delos Studio

Library of Congress Cataloging-in-Publication Data

Al-Malood, Fawaz
        The Hotel Industry: A High Turnover Industry

Library of Congress Control Number: 2023912988

Paperback ISBN: 979-8-9885484-0-9
E-book ISBN: 979-8-9885484-1-6

Printed in the United States of America

Disclaimer

This book is provided "as is" without any representations or warranties, expressed or implied. The author makes no representations or warranties about the information included in this book.

Nothing in this book constitutes or is meant to constitute advice of any kind. The views expressed in this book are those of the author, alone, and should not be taken as expert advice or instructions. The information and strategies stated in this book may not work for everyone, and readers are urged to do their due diligence to determine whether the suggestions and strategies listed are appropriate, permissible, and legal in the organization and locality they are in. Readers are responsible for their actions.

The author does not assume any liability to the reader or purchaser (whether under the law of contract, the law of torts, or otherwise) about the contents of, the use of, or otherwise in connection with this book.

Dedication

This book is dedicated to all the amazing individuals who work so tirelessly in the hotel industry to make someone else's life more comfortable and memorable.

May your work be recognized, may your load be lightened, and may you be generously rewarded for all that you do.

Preface

This book started as a research study that I worked on over twenty years ago. I was a professional hotelier who loved my field and was looking forward to a long and exciting career in hotel management. However, I was appalled by the high employee turnover rate in hotels that I witnessed, and I wanted to get to the root causes that led people to quit.

I had intended to publish my findings in a book, but I never got around to converting my manuscript into a book until now. At the time I conducted my research, the internet was young, and few books, articles, and resources addressed this topic. Today, while more literature has been published on this topic, and the problem has been studied and written about in peer-reviewed journals, the problem persists. The hotel industry still suffers from high turnover and some hotel companies still have no clue why their employees quit or what to do about it. Interestingly, the data that I share in his book is still relevant.

I hope that what I have learned through my research and published in this book will help current hoteliers with significant voluntary employee turnover get a better grip on the problem and develop appropriate solutions. The hotel industry is a challenging one, but it can be a rewarding one as well. By creating a positive and productive work environment for their employees, hoteliers can attract and retain the best talent, which will lead to a better bottom line.

Table of Contents

Chapter One:
Introduction

Years ago, I worked at a large resort hotel in one of the busiest tourist destinations in the world, Orlando, Florida. I loved the hotel industry! I loved the hustle and bustle, I loved meeting new people from around the world every day, I loved finding ways to make the guest experience a memorable one, and I loved finding ways to contribute to the success of my team and the company I worked for.

I wasn't a newbie to the hotel industry, but Florida was my new home and one of several cities that I had lived in. By the time I moved to Florida, I had already earned degrees from Switzerland and the U.S. in Hotel Management. I had lived on three continents, and had worked for several four- and five-star hotels, as well as the airline catering division of an airport service company.

Regardless of where I had moved to and worked, the one constant was the employees. Many of them, including the managers, were career hoteliers. Most of the people I had met and worked with internationally chose to be hoteliers, they typically joined a company, stuck with it for years, and moved through the ranks. A few of them moved around to other companies, but it was typically due to an opportunity for promotion. However, most of the people I encountered were loyal to a particular brand or employer. My first General Manager, for instance, was a Greek gentleman who shared with me that he started as a Pool Boy at the Hilton Athens in Greece decades ago. It was a low-skill, entry-level position, but with persistence, hard work, and professional development, he gradually began rising to higher positions. When I met him, he was in his mid-fifties and the General Manager of a 5-star Hilton Hotel receiving a generous salary, and excellent benefits. His story was similar to virtually every manager I had met in the industry. They all started in entry-level positions, and by dedicating themselves to their profession and the company they joined, they found a life-long, mutually beneficial working relationship.

Employee turnover was low, less than 50 %, at the various hotel companies that I had interned with or worked at. I only knew of one instance where an employee was terminated by the hotel for lack of punctuality. He was unable to show up to work on time, and after going through the progressive discipline process, he was let go.

Things were different in the United States. I had been at my Florida resort hotel for nine months, and I was shocked at the employee turnover rate within my department, the Front Office Department. I had previously lived and worked in places where most people joined a company and stayed there until they retired. I was not used to seeing people quit after a few months with such frequency. It seemed unnatural to me, and extremely expensive for the hotel companies that had to recruit, replace, and train someone new so frequently. I was flabbergasted, so I decided to chronicle what I was witnessing and study the cause of this seemingly high turnover rate.

Why study voluntary employee turnover?

Employees are typically the largest expense on a hotel's budget, which makes them the most valuable resource. So, would it then not make sense to assume that the industry would do whatever it could to protect its resources and invest in its growth?

The hotel industry has one of the worst employee turnover rates known within any customer services industry.

Typically, the turnover rate within the hotel industry ranges between 70%-130% annually, although higher departmental rates have been known to reach up to 300% (Woods, 2012).

Personal work experience inspired my curiosity to learn more about the phenomenal employee turnover in the hotel industry.

The following table lists the positions within the front office department at my Florida resort hotel, the number of staff occupying each position, and the turnover rate for each position.

Table 1. Front Office Turnover Rate

Position	No. of staff	Turnover	Turnover rate
Front Office Manager	1	3	300%
Assistant Front Office Manager	3	2	67%
Rooms Coordinator	1	3	300%
Night Audit Manager	1	1	100%
Assistant Night Audit Manager	1	1	100%
Night Auditor	1	4	400%
Guest Service Agent	10	1	10%
*PBX Operator	3	6	200%
Bell Desk	3	4	133%

*PBX: (Private Business Exchange). Statistics are based on a nine-month period.

Based on the data presented in Table 1, the turnover rate of six out of the nine positions listed far surpassed the typical turnover rate within the hotel industry. While the reasons for the turnover in each position varied and involved more than simply one factor, they all combined several of the following reasons:

1. Training
2. Money

3. Working Conditions
4. Incompetence
5. Pressure/Stress

Lack of training was the most common reason among all the departing employees. This hotel did not have a formal training system or procedure for any position. None of the employees received proper or structured training. Most of them seemed to have been thrown into their positions without a mentor, trainer, or even guidelines to follow. New managers were briefed on the problems facing the department and simply expected to perform miracles and change things around. Line-level employees, such as PBX operators and servers, were paired with more senior employees for a day or two to "show them the ropes" and serve as their trainers. The expectation was that the new employee would learn all the policies and procedures pertaining to their assigned area in a few days. However, no written instructions were provided, and no monitoring or evaluation was done. Additionally, none of the "supposed" trainers were qualified to train nor versed in the principles of instructing and relaying information to trainees. They just happened to be folks who had been there longer than anyone. When asked, none of them had ever seen a Standard Operating Procedure (SOP) for their department or job aide.

The result was that, in most cases, new employees were not able to perform all their duties efficiently or completely. Consequently, employees felt frustrated for not knowing how to do their jobs and felt pressured since they were still held accountable for their performance. Realizing this, most employees simply quit to explore other employment opportunities that offered proper training and higher compensation.

What some managers fail to realize is that training, among other factors, is as important an incentive and motivator to employees as money, bonuses, and promotions.

Discovery Journey

As I embarked on my discovery journey, I wanted to learn about the factors that resulted in voluntary employee turnover in the hotel industry. In doing so, I wanted to answer the following questions:

1. Why do people join the hotel industry?
2. Why do some people stay, while others quit?
3. What hotel departments experience the highest turnover rates?
4. What are the top 10 reasons hotel employees quit?
5. What solutions do hoteliers and human resources departments propose to reduce voluntary employee turnover?

While the specific reason for employee turnover varies in each case, I aimed to acquire sufficient data to determine if there was a common denominator or common and repetitive reasons. The data gathered would identify areas that need to be addressed to increase employee retention.

Additionally, while some of my hotelier colleagues attributed the turnover to the lower wages offered in the hotel industry, I knew that there were other employers, such as the U.S. Army, that also offered comparable low wages but had a much higher retention of enlisted personnel, even after their enlistment period was over. I wanted to learn what they did to maintain low employee turnover rates.

In chapter three, I'll discuss what I learned from the U.S. Army after spending time surveying and interviewing Army Recruiters.

Chapter Two:
The Effects of Employee Turnover

"Finding and keeping employees has never been easy. But now, full employment has converged with a service and information economy, making recruitment and retention the most pressing challenge facing American business today."
-J. W. Marriott, Jr.

Employee turnover is a destructive phenomenon that occurs naturally in every organization. It is destructive because it disrupts the operational functionality of an organization. Turnover increases the workload of remaining employees who are needed to make up for the loss of human-power, which inadvertently increases stress and decreases morale. Employee turnover also increases administrative costs since human resources departments need to recruit, hire, and train a replacement for the departing employee. More explicitly, employee turnover results in a loss of resources. Time, money, human resources, and clientele are all resources that are lost as a result of voluntary turnover.

Organizations lose time due to decreased productivity from the loss of an employee and through the organizations' efforts in recruiting, hiring, and training replacements for departed employees. Consequently, loss of time results in loss of money (revenue) through the cost of replacement. A *Wall Street Journal* article estimates the cost of replacing an employee to be roughly one-and-a-half times a year's pay (Ashby & Pell, 2001).

Furthermore, when an employee resigns, the burden of completing their duties is often assigned to the remaining employees, which may overload them with undesired responsibilities, pressure, and stress. Eventually, this encourages the remaining employees to consider better employment opportunities with other employers.

Organizations will lose their client base that may not be comfortable with constantly having to deal with new employees or may notice a decline in quality or customer services because of turnover.

When turnover reaches percentage rates that are as high as those within the hotel industry, which often exceed 100%, it can be a malignant disease that eats away at the potential of an organization to grow, improve, and succeed. While there are no remedies to cure this Human Resources Cancer (employee turnover), the possibility to control and reduce the growth of this disease does exist. In the medical field, the treatment of disease begins with understanding the causes of the illness. Therefore, to develop solutions to control voluntary terminations, we need to be able to identify the reasons that result in voluntary employee turnover in the hotel industry.

Identifying the factors that result in voluntary turnover is a step toward exploring new methods and processes to treat the problem. This lays a foundation from which employers can initiate a genuine effort to preserve their most valuable assets, employees.

Many organizations and managers have misconceptions regarding the nature of the real problem that leads to turnover. The two researchers previously cited, Ashby & Pell, investigated turnover and concluded that the sources of the problem can be attributed directly to *Corporate Culture*. The correlation between employee turnover and corporate culture prescribes that employers that have relatively low turnover attracted favorable applicants, built loyalty, and possessed a "corporate culture that cultivated latent, interest and strength of employees".

Ashby & Pell also found that "companies with the highest turnover rates are those in which corporate culture is one of domination, autocracy, and inflexibility." Regardless of what those companies had to offer in terms of compensation and incentives, good employees will still leave.

High turnover is an indicator that employees are dissatisfied with their jobs. Though reasons for turnover vary on an individual basis, low morale is a prime culprit in many cases (Handelsman, 1998).

Most good employees leave companies due to the circumstances and situations created by management that create an undesirable corporate culture. Therefore, Smith (2001) pointed out that management is to be held responsible for turnover. To combat the problem, Smith encourages organizations to develop what he calls a "retentionship program" that effervesces eight key elements that will turn an organization from a high turnover company to a high retention company. These elements are:

1. A clear sense of direction and purpose
2. Caring management
3. Flexible benefits and schedules adapted to the needs of individuals
4. Open communication
5. A charged work environment
6. Performance management
7. Reward and recognition
8. Training and development

Smith also emphasizes the importance of effective leadership that creates a productive work environment through exercising "soft management skills." Smith states, "I believe soft management skills-people skills are the critical element in battling high turnover and creating a culture of retentionship".

The Saratoga Institute reports that 50% of work environment satisfaction is determined by the relationship employees have with their boss. Likewise, a Gallup poll showed that the majority of employees valued having a caring boss more than they valued money or fringe benefits (Ashby & Pell, 2001).

A workforce retention survey conducted by Smith indicated that 35% of employees quit their previous jobs due to the attitude of their direct supervisors or managers.

Handelsman (1998) on the other hand presented a more detailed case that high turnover results from some of the following reasons:

1. A bad match between the employee's skills and the job.
2. Employees who are placed in jobs that are too difficult for them or whose skills are underutilized may become discouraged and quit. Inadequate information about skill requirements that are needed to fill a job may result in the hiring of either under-skilled or overqualified workers.
3. Substandard equipment, tools, or facilities. If working conditions are substandard or the workplace lacks important facilities, such as proper lighting, furniture, clean restrooms, and other health and safety provisions, employees won't be willing to put up with the inconvenience for long.
4. Lack of opportunity for advancement or growth. The job should be described precisely, without

raising false hopes for growth and advancement in the position.

5. Feelings of not being appreciated. Since employees generally want to do a good job, it follows that they also want to be appreciated and recognized for their work. Even the most seasoned employee needs to be told what he or she is doing right once in a while.

6. Inadequate or lackluster supervision and training. Employees need guidance and direction. New employees may need extra help in learning an unfamiliar job. Similarly, the absence of a training program may cause workers to fall behind in their level of performance and feel that their abilities are lacking.

7. Unequal or substandard wage structures. When two or more employees perform similar work and have similar responsibilities, differences in pay rate can drive lower paid employees to quit. In a like vein, if you pay less than other employers for similar work, employees are likely to jump ship for higher pay, if other factors are relatively equal.

Furthermore, Handelsman identifies two categories of factors that lead to voluntary turnover, those two categories being internal factors and external factors. He contends that organizations are very limited in exercising any action that would prevent good employees from leaving. The external factors include: "family responsibility, financial obligation, marketability of skills, and jobs offered by other companies." Fortunately, organizations can control internal factors that lead good employees to leave. These factors include: "benefits, compensation, pleasant working conditions, opportunities for growth/advancement, and job security".

Kirby D. Payne (1998) former President of a Minneapolis-based American Hospitality Management Company admits that though he does not have the real answer to the turnover problem that plagues the hotel industry, he feels that the problem may be controlled and minimized with the implementation of "all the good ideas one reads and hears about." Payne states that managers need to question themselves in three critical areas to be able to determine where they failed in their efforts to retain employees.

The first area is hiring; managers need to ask themselves if they should have hired that person in the first place. Managers also need to do a thorough background check on employees. Organizations such as Trans Union and AVERT, provide credit checks, workers-compensation histories, education confirmation, previous employment verification, and driving records for employers. Performing these background checks and informing applicants that you perform them automatically "weeds out" unsuitable applicants (Payne, 1998).

The second area is training. According to Kennedy & Berger (1994), a contributing factor to employee turnover in hotels seems to be the one-dimensional focus of their orientation programs. Employees encounter feelings of uncertainty about the unknown whenever they accept promotions or transfers, but the greatest stress and uncertainty come when they accept a new job with a new employer. For that reason, orientation programs should deal with both the emotional and the informational needs of new hires. A look at the orientation programs of six hotels found many similarities among the programs. Their initial component extended from one-and-a-half to five days in length, with few programs having additional orientation follow-ups after 12, 60, or 90 days. All but one included specific information about the new employee's department along with general information about the organization. But only one property had the express purpose of reducing new employees' anxiety and thereby turnover.

Following a guided orientation plan designed to both familiarize new employees with aspects of a hotel and build relationships with the newcomers, reduces turnover. A personable orientation and detailed action plan can build trust and are motivating (Belilos, 1999).

Employers are encouraged to investigate the reasons that drive new hires away a few days after joining a company by determining if the new employees were overwhelmed or were not presented with all the facts and information they needed to know about their assumed responsibilities.

The third and final area discussed by Payne is leadership. He defines leadership as the "balance of positive and negative feedback tailored for that individual." The author envisions a leader as someone who can apply judgment to employees. Bearing in mind that each employee receives and perceives information differently, Payne draws a picture of a leader as a person who can craft directives and provide feedback, incentives, and training equally and reasonably to accommodate the needs of staff. Utilizing a combination of variables to create a retention program is essential since there is no single element that will cure the turnover problem.

Like Payne, Dr. Alan Stutts, former Dean of Conrad Hilton College at the University of Houston, also highlights three-problem areas in the hotel industry that contribute to the growing turnover rates. Stutts (2001) noted that hiring, training and promotion are frequently the crisis areas primarily due to the fact that hospitality recruiters seldom use effective and precise selective measurement tools. Stutts suggests that hiring through resumes, references, and interviews is inadequate. He justifies this by saying that resumes can be easily falsified or misrepresented, and business references rarely reveal any beneficial information regarding the attributes or skills of a potential employee. In reference to training, Stutts states that the "one size fits all approach...has failed to provide the desired results." More often than not, excellent employees that have been promoted have performed poorly because they have not been equipped with the skills to make "people decisions".

Stutts' solution in addressing the weakness in hiring, training, and promoting, is to utilize assessments. Assessments produce remarkable results in identifying and selecting the right candidates or employees for the right job. Four assessments are mentioned by Stutts: the Sales Indicator, the Performance Indicator, the Profile, and the Step One Survey. Developed by Assessment Center Inc., these assessments are designed to identify desired characteristics and traits in potential and current employees. The results of the assessments allegedly provide an objective analysis and summary for pre-hire candidates and current employees being considered for promotions. Based on the results, intelligent hiring decisions can be made using scientific measurement tools for job matching.

Hiring is an area that needs to be addressed to reduce turnover. Shanahan (2000), notes that hospitality recruiters and employers are guilty of adhering to antiquated hiring practices, which are preventing good prospective employees from joining and are encouraging the current good employees to leave as a result of being surrounded by incompetent people.

In an article titled *Recruit and Hire Differently, Reduce Turnover, and Save Lots of Money* by Shanahan, the writer narrates how many employers misinterpret the word "experience", and view it as a statement that a person is an *expert* at what they do. While that may be true in some cases, quite often it is not applicable. The fact that a person has experience does not necessarily exemplify them as an expert. Shanahan states, "Whether they have been on the job for thirty days or thirty years, poorly trained service persons with bad habits and little motivation still provide poor service. We should not ignore work experience but rather not assume that applicants are skilled because they have experience" (2000).

Chapter Three:
The Army's Way of Reducing Turnover

While the hotel industry faces many challenges in recruiting, hiring, training, and retaining qualified staff, it is not alone in its dilemma. The U.S. Army also faces similar challenges; however, the U.S. Army has devised a system that has worked well for them in their human resources challenges. Their efforts have resulted in higher retention and lower turnover rates. The following section is dedicated to examining the methods used by the U.S. Army in achieving its recruitment and retention goals.

Recruitment

There are many misconceptions about joining the U.S. Army that makes recruiting for them quite a challenge. Some of these misconceptions include:

1. One who joins the U.S. Army is going to be shipped off to fight a war.
2. It does not pay to join the Army because of low pay and benefits, which is why you see a lot of homeless veterans on the streets.
3. Living a military lifestyle is difficult because they have so many rules.

Contrary to those beliefs, the Army is far from being simply a combat organization with an underpaid personnel body. The U.S. Army offers enlisted personnel: over 200 jobs fields to choose from, the most comprehensive and generous education tuition assistance, the flexibility to choose where you want to relocate (upon availability), an enlistment bonus, and 30 days paid vacation annually. It is virtually impossible to find a corporate organization that can meet the benefits offered by the U.S. Army for entry-level and young recruits.

Though the Army finds it difficult to sign up recruits, they do not necessarily accept everyone that walks through their door with the intention of becoming a soldier. Filling positions with warm bodies is not the Army's policy. As with any professional organization, the U.S. Army ensures the suitability of its applicant pool by qualifying them. Applicants must meet certain requirements before recruitment. All applicants are required to fill out the standard application and take designated tests. U.S. Army recruiters screen and investigate applicants who must provide references, good history, and provide family information. Applicants are also asked moral questions (U.S. Army, 2001).

Selection

The U.S. Army offers more than 200 fields of specialties, from combat forces to electronics engineering, and even medical positions. To ensure enlisted personnel are selected for the jobs they are best suited for, the Army requires each recruit to take a test called the Armed Services Vocational Aptitude Battery (ASVAB). This is a series of 10 sub-tests designed to help determine one's potential for Army training and job placement.

Based on the results of the ASVAB, recruits may select from different job categories for which they qualify. Recruits are also made aware of the availability of vacancies for the jobs they are interested in and the location of the desired job.

Training

Training for the Army may be categorized into two types of required training: Basic Training and Advanced Individual Training.

Basic Training, also referred to as Boot Camp, which all recruits are required to attend is a 9-week process that conditions enlisted personnel both physically and psychologically. During the 9-week Basic Training all participants receive the core values and training that constitute a soldier. The intent of the training is to bring the "body and mind to peak levels" (U.S. Army).

Advanced Individual Training (AIT) is designed to train soldiers for the specific jobs they choose. A combination of classroom instruction and hands-on training methodology is applied to deliver the best individualized training available. AIT generally runs from a month to a year, depending on the nature and complexity of the job being trained for.

To ensure that every candidate attains the desired skills and level of efficiency, the army utilizes a consequential progression phase system. No candidate is permitted to progress from one phase to another unless they achieve the skills required and are efficient in them.

On-The-Job

Military trainers and leaders attend a Professional Leadership Development Course (PLDC), which allows them to operate efficiently in positions of command, training, or counseling. Maintaining healthy levels of morale is fundamental to establishing a productive work environment. The U.S. Army creates a healthy level of morale by providing appraisals, positive reinforcement, encouragement, and by rewarding personnel. The PLDC is significant in the success of improved morale.

The military established a simplistic form of communication between officers and enlisted personnel. Everything passes through a chain of command. Commanders and unit leaders meet their supporting officers where they provide them with information that needs to be communicated to personnel. Much like the corporate world, information travels from top-to-bottom and vice versa.

Turnover

As with any field and industry, the Army also experiences turnover; however, its turnover rate is approximately 29% (Chetri, 2021). In comparison to the hotel industry, turnover in the Army is low.

The reason for turnover in the U.S. Army varies from person to person. According to an Army recruiter at the El Monte Recruiting Station in California, people join the Army for different reasons with varying goals. Once those goals are met, some personnel decide to leave. For example, the military provides excellent educational benefits, and that is a reason why some people join the Army. Joining the Army allows them to accomplish a personal goal of earning a college degree, which they typically may not be able to afford on their own. All enlisted members with high-school diplomas are guaranteed admission to hundreds of federally funded colleges or universities. Furthermore, the Army will pay 100% of an enlisted member's tuition fees while in service. The Army also provides free laptops computers and Internet access to personnel studying through distance learning programs. To top it off, each member receives college money once they leave or retire from the Army for tuition fees. The amount allocated varies from approximately $23,000 up to $50,000 depending on preset eligibility. Therefore, for many, joining the Army for 2 years or even 4 years is an excellent method of funding their educational prospects.

Others may join the Army to learn certain marketable skills, which they can benefit from once they complete their enlistment contract. These skills may include telecommunication technology, broadcasting, navigation, paramedic training, water treatment, aircraft maintenance, and many others that could be used in civilian society. Joining the Army also provides the opportunity to travel, experience other cultures, and live abroad.

Retention

Enlisting in the U.S. Army is by no means a lifetime commitment, as people can enlist in the Army for as little as 2 years. Enlisted personnel are eligible and are encouraged to re-enlist once their original enlistment period is over.

Recruiting and training personnel to be proficient in the jobs they are hired for is a costly operation. It is commonly known that it is far less costly to retain a current employee than to hire and train a new one. Realizing this the U.S. Army exercises exhaustive methods and incentives to maximize retention and reduce turnover to a minimum. For instance, military retention counselors meet with enlisted personnel who are about to complete their enlistment period to discuss what the soldiers' plans are. Counselors attempt to identify what soldiers are looking for and assist them in locating it within the army. If a soldier is interested in a change of jobs, relocating, or furthering their education or career aspects, the Retention Counselors will work towards providing those options to soldiers to encourage them to reenlist. The U.S. Army also provides monetary re-enlistment incentives that vary depending on a soldier's qualifications. In one case, a soldier who was an electronics expert based in Virginia considered rejoining civilian society, and relocating back to his native state, California, as his enlistment period approached its end. To encourage his re-enlistment, the military relocated him to California and gave him an $8,000 re-enlistment bonus.

Hospitality in Relation to the U.S. Army

While the hotel industry may not be able to be as generous when it comes to providing monetary incentives to retain good employees, it can certainly learn how recruitment, organization, structured training, clear communications, and leadership can result in reducing turnover to a manageable rate, as it has for the U.S. Army. Both the hotel industry and the military are known for their nominal wages. Yet the military has surpassed the hotel industry in being an employer of choice by looking for good candidates, training them, treating them with respect and dignity, and providing them with the tools and equipment needed for them to perform to their optimum potential.

Most of the elements needed to improve employees' performance and increase retention are already within hospitality companies' grasp; they can be found in corporate policies, procedures, and training manuals, which were designed to enhance the effectiveness of their operation and provide a favorable and productive work environment. Unfortunately, many hotels fail to implement and utilize these established procedures. Others fail to even look at the guides they set for themselves.

Chapter Four:
Hierarchy of Employee Needs

In a market with an ample supply of providers, consumers are privileged with the option of selecting products and services that are consistent with their needs and wants. People have a perception of what they consider to be a valuable product or service. That perception defines the level of quality in the eyes of consumers. Consumers define quality based on several criteria, some of which include necessity, taste, usefulness, and alignment with personal financial flexibility.

Suppliers in any free market constantly compete to produce better products at reasonable prices to outperform competitors. The goal is to increase market size, which would ultimately increase revenue, profitability, and growth.

In the hotel industry, employees need to be identified as consumers and valuable resources. A common quote that circulates in the industry and is attributed to Edgar Mitchell is, "If we don't take care of our customers, someone else will."

This quote is also applicable to employees. Employees are consumers; they have needs, wants, and demands. As consumers, they are fortunate enough to be in an industry with an ample variety of suppliers (employers) to pick from. If a current employer cannot or will not meet their needs, many others will. Just as companies compete to create, steal, and retain customers, they need to work just as hard to find, satisfy, and retain employees.

A restaurant may create the most delicious meals, which are sold at reasonable prices and served professionally in a pleasant and comfortable environment; however, if they do not work just as hard to serve employees with the same effort and dedication, soon the first customers to walk out the doors would be the internal customers, followed by the external customers who will be disappointed with the inconsistent service caused by employee turnover.

Employees are living resources that companies use to produce services and products in exchange for an agreed-upon wage, benefits, and acceptable working conditions. In a sense, employees to companies are a means to an end, much like machines and robots. Machines will produce services or products in exchange for energy and proper maintenance. Machines are, however, much simpler resources to manage when compared to human beings.

Machines have no feelings; they express no emotions, require no breaks or vacations, and all shifts are convenient working hours. A well-maintained machine will not stop producing consistent products or services if we yell at them or have them work odd hours, nor will they seek better employment opportunities. Employers need to acknowledge the fact that they cannot simply expect all employees to be dedicated, loyal, or hardworking, or to constantly produce at optimum levels simply because we pay them. Human beings are much more complex in that they respond to a multitude of stimuli cumulatively and constantly. Employers need to remember that, unlike machines, employees are human beings and are driven by needs and emotions. To achieve the desired response from employees we must identify the needs of employees within the hotel industry as Abraham Maslow identified the needs of humans in society. If we were to adapt Maslow's Hierarchy of Needs (Table 2) to the needs of employees within a workplace, it would look like this.

Table 2. Maslow Hierarchy Adapted to Employees

	Hierarchy of Employee Needs

1	*Physical Work Environment Needs:*
	• Safe and comfortable work environment
	• Suitable physical conditions:
	  • temperature and humidity
	  • suitable uniforms/dress code
	  • pleasant aesthetics
	• Training
	• Supply of necessary tools and equipment

2	*Job Security & Stability Needs:* • Performing duties without the fear of termination or layoff • Predictable schedules • Financial stability • Opportunities for growth and development

3	*Emotional Needs:*
	• Employees need to feel that their employers are:
	  • understanding of their professional and personal needs
	  • compassionate to their unique individual situations
	  • caring

4	*Self-Pride and Satisfaction Needs:* • Satisfaction with jobs, duties performed, and recognition received
5	*Self-Actualization Needs:* • Professional/Career Contentment • Aspiration and involvement in developing other employees' and the industry

Analyzing the Hierarchy of Employee Needs

1. Physical Work Environment:

Comfortable Work Area

Many job types exist within the hotel industry. Each job type defines the architecture and logistics of the work area for any given position. For instance, while a doorman's position requires him to stand on his feet outdoors all day; a telephone operator is required to be seated indoors all day. Understanding the physical demands of each job is imperative for employers to address employees' "Physical Work Environment Needs." If we examine a doorman's position closely, we learn that it is physically demanding. A doorman is on his feet all day and is expected to maintain a professional posture for very little monetary compensation. If employers do not provide doormen with comfortable shoes, uniforms, and regular breaks to alleviate some of the physical exhaustion and stress caused by the work environment, eventually their doormen will find other jobs. Employers silently provide employees with reasons to quit by ignoring the significance of providing an adequate, acceptable, and comfortable physical work environment.

Pleasant Aesthetics

We all would love to have a nice job where we feel comfortable physically and with the aesthetics. A common practice by employees found virtually everywhere is filling work areas with things of significance to them. For instance, while some people enjoy posting pictures of family, friends, quotes, or relaxing scenery, others may prefer to surround their area with toys, soft toys, or other trinkets.

While this may not be appropriate for each employee due to the type of job and physical location (i.e., outdoor locations, public-facing areas, front of the house, and shared spaces) employers need to be considerate of the importance of aesthetics in motivating and encouraging productivity.

Studies have repeatedly demonstrated that the color pink has a calming and soothing effect on people (Carey, 2002). So why should we not identify other stimuli that have positive effects on employees?

Suitable Work Conditions

Most mid to large hotel companies provide uniforms to employees who are in direct contact with customers. While the brand alignment of uniforms is a factor to be reasonably considered, the quality of the uniforms issued to employees is of higher significance. When selecting uniforms, employers should consider the following criteria:

1. Aesthetics: Uniforms should be consistent with the general theme and colors of the company while remaining in good taste.

2. Durability: The fabric used should be resilient, able to withstand daily use, washing, pressing, and still maintain its shape and color.

3. Comfort & Functionality: This is probably the least considered factor by employers when designing and ordering uniforms, although it may be the most important one. Numerous corporate companies allow employees to dress casually on certain days or every day. People like being comfortable when performing any task. When employees are comfortable, they are much more relaxed and productive in their jobs. Imagine what the results of surgery would be if surgeons were required to wear formal attire in the operating room. I would have to assume that surgeons would not be too focused on their surgery because they're preoccupied with how uncomfortable and restricting their clothing is for the tasks they are performing. This is why surgeons wear comfortable scrubs in the operating room. So just as comfortable clothing is important to surgeons in saving lives, comfortable clothing to employees could be important in remaining in a job. Therefore, when ordering and designing uniforms, employers should evaluate the comfort and functionality of uniforms for different jobs. For instance, while a long coat, gloves, and a hat seem ideal for a doorman in Massachusetts in November due to the cooler weather where the temperatures range from the mid-30s to mid-50s, it is not appropriate for an employee performing the same duties in Florida where the temperature is warmer and ranges from the mid-70s to low 80s.

Supply of Necessary Tools and Equipment

A carpenter needs his hammers, nails, and saw to build furniture; likewise, hotel employees need to have adequate and appropriate tools to provide quick, efficient, and consistent service to guests. A front desk agent, for instance, requires an updated computer and software, which would allow them to perform their duties in an effective and timely manner. A food server requires sufficient menus, trays, cutlery, and crockery. Employers must provide each employee with all the tools and equipment that they require. Employees find it frustrating to work in an environment where they lack the very resources that allow them to complete their jobs.

Years ago, I worked at a hotel where the housekeeping department did not have enough linen inventory to replenish the rooms. The hotel was supposed to have a bare minimum par stock of 3 for linen.

The 3-par stock system is a method of managing linen inventory in a hotel. It ensures that there is always enough linen available to meet the needs of guests, while also minimizing the amount of linen that is in storage. The system works by having three sets of linens for each guest room: one set is in use by guests, one set is being laundered and processed, and one set is folded and placed in the linen closet or storage to be used once the guest room is stripped of its dirty linen after use. This is a cyclical linen inventory management process that ensures that there is always a clean set of linens available for guests.

However, this particular hotel operated on a par stock of 1.5. The result was that many rooms were missing towels or could not be sold on time because they were missing pillowcases or bed sheets. This caused some employees to take matters into their own hands and hoard the limited inventory of linen so that they could do their jobs, which meant that other employees never had enough linen for the rooms they were responsible for cleaning. This led to employee frustration and dissatisfaction, guest complaints, loss of revenue, and increased costs in the laundry department, which now had to operate overtime to wash the limited linen inventory available.

Employers should not expect employees to simply get by. Employees cannot produce services and products for sale if they do not have the proper resources. They cannot give what they do not have.

2. Job Security and Stability Needs:

Termination

Employee performance is either positively or negatively determined by their psychological state of mind. In other words, an employee's mood could define the output of his or her performance. Therefore, an employee needs to be in a pleasant state of mind to perform well in the hotel industry. If employees constantly feel that their employment is in danger of being terminated, they are naturally going to be suffering constantly from anxiety, stress, and depression. Negative emotions such as these directly affect an employer in two ways.

The first way is through poor employee service. An employee's performance and potential are obstructed, which results in the lowering of standards and guest dissatisfaction.

The second is through an increase in employee turnover, as well as the cost of hiring new employees.

Employees need to be able to go to work without having to worry about whether or not they will be "let go". Who wants to work for an employer who does not value his or her employees nor provide a nurturing and supportive environment? Probably no one! Yet, unfortunately, there are still employers who use termination as a tool to force employees to produce. This scare tactic that some employers use is a threat that employees do not appreciate. What these employers do not realize is that these termination threats create disloyalty and drive employees away since they violate one of the basic needs in a job for employees, the need for Job Security.

Financial Security and Stability

Employees are regular people with responsibilities and commitments to uphold outside the workplace. Most of these responsibilities are financial such as the cost of rent, utility bills, transportation, food, clothing, and other expenses. In order to meet these financial responsibilities, employees need some level of financial security and stability.

Employers need to make a commitment to employees by securing the number of hours that employees are promised at the time of hire. Employers also need to dispense wages accurately and on schedule without delay. Hotel jobs are notorious for paying extremely low wages. Most hotel employees live paycheck to paycheck and cannot afford to have inaccuracies or delays with their wages.

Although money is not always a motivator to apply for a new job, it certainly is an attractive incentive. Jack Welch, former CEO and Chairman of General Electric, best addressed this issue with this statement when questioned about recognition and money: "You have to get rewarded in your soul and the wallet. The money isn't enough, but a plaque isn't enough either" (Peters, 2002). With the billions of dollars in revenue and profit that are pumped into the hotel industry, employers should pay employees better than the traditional minimum wage. Unfortunately, that is not the case. Hotel companies often complain about the problem they have with the turnover due to employees who leave for better-paying jobs, as well as the poor quality of applicants they receive. One factor that can address that problem would be to increase wages.

What kind of employees do hotel companies expect to get and keep if they have employees working physically and emotionally demanding jobs for minimum wage or close to minimum wage? The answer to that question lies in an old English proverb that goes something like this, "If you pay peanuts, you get monkeys".

If you pay "minimum" wage, expect to get "minimum" quality and performance. When employers offer competitive wages, they are in a superior position to:

1. Expect and attract a higher caliber of applicants.
2. Earn the loyalty and commitment of current employees, who will no longer be on the lookout for higher-paying jobs with other companies.

Employees feel undervalued and unappreciated for their hard work when paid low wages. At times, employees even feel insulted and exploited when they receive a negligible wage increase.

A regular practice at one company was to award salary raises at the end of each year to employees who performed well. Typically, that would be regarded as a commendable practice; however, in some cases, it may be interpreted otherwise by employees depending on the amount of compensation offered.

In one case, a worker filed a grievance for inhumane treatment. The worker had received a salary raise in recognition of his laborious efforts that equated to $2.65 a month. His so-called raise was 8 cents a day.

Similarly, at a 4-star hotel, a Reservations Supervisor received a monthly raise of a mere $1.32 in recognition of her efforts. While these employers might commend themselves for the fact that they have a reward system that recognizes outstanding employees, in reality the employees in both of these cases felt insulted, undervalued, and unappreciated for receiving such an insignificant raise. The so-called raises weren't even enough to cover the cost of a full meal for one person at a fast-food restaurant.

Promise and Growth

Another factor that falls under Job Security Needs is the need for growth within the company. Certain employees are comfortable doing the same job every day for the rest of their careers. Predominantly, employees, especially younger ones, aspire to climb the corporate ladder into higher positions. This need for growth should be addressed by employers for each employee. Employers need to:

1. Learn what each employee's career aspirations and goals are.
2. Determine if the employee's goals are attainable and consistent with the company's operation.
3. Outline a development path that will help employees reach their goals.

3. Emotional Needs:

Newton's Third Law of Motion states that "For every action, there is an equal and opposite reaction." Though this law is taught mainly in science classes, it applies to everything in life, including human psychology.

The things we say to people, and the way our message is delivered, solicit the type of response we get from them. Employees react to their jobs, employers, and coworkers based on the way they are treated. Treat them with dignity, respect, kindness, appreciation, and enthusiasm, and they flourish. Treat them with incivility, and performance, productivity, quality, and more importantly loyalty suffer.

A Harvard study showed that the cost of incivility runs into the millions as employees subjected to incivility in the workplace respond by being less committed to the employer, reducing their effort and quality of work, reflecting their frustrations on customers, and quitting (Levin, 2018).

Studies have also shown that when employees are unhappy with their employers, they will react in several ways to express their dissatisfaction. Table 3 provides a list of how employees react when satisfied and dissatisfied.

Table 3. Employee Responses: Satisfied vs Dissatisfied

Satisfied	Dissatisfied
Emotionally (Enthusiasm)	Emotionally (Depression, resentment)
Verbally (Appraisals)	Verbally (Complaints)
Physically (Higher productivity & performance)	Physically (Poor performance and productivity)
Attendance (Coming to work early)	Attendance (Tardiness and absences)
Taking initiative (going the extra mile)	Aggressively (Damage property/equipment)
Follow directions and accept feedback	Incompliance/insubordination

Employees are human beings. They need to be nurtured, loved, and cared for to get the best out of them. While an authoritarian management style may get the results they need from employees in the short term, in the long run, it adversely causes the loss of many good employees, due to lack of human emotional attention. On the other hand, while supporting and nurturing corporate culture require more time to harness the potential of each employee, in the long run, it is those that do who succeed in maintaining a healthy, happy, and productive workforce with minimal turnover.

We do not need to look far to define the emotional needs that employees require; we simply need to look at the much-needed nurturing and support we provide children. New junior employees are like young children when they join a new company or department—not in a pejorative sense, but in a humanistic sense.

In the beginning, they are very vulnerable and require a lot of love, support, attention, and guidance. Soon enough, they will be able to stand on their own two feet. As children grow older, wiser, and increasingly self-reliant, they may not need as much direct attention as they did in their first few years. However, they need to know that it is there for them when they need it, no matter how much they grow.

Likewise, new employees need all the love, support, and guidance they can receive from employers, if employers want to set them up for success. Ideally speaking a trainer or mentor should be assigned to new employees full-time until their training is complete, and they feel confident enough to fly solo.

A 1979 study on mentoring by two fellows of the Sloan School of Management at M.I.T affirms that having a mentor lends to the success of employees in organizations. Their research included interviews with highly successful individuals such as Nobel laureates, corporate president and vice presidents, and other accomplished individuals. They state that, "Mentoring has existed in organizations and professions for many years" and that "people need a mentor in order to *make it* in an organization" (Davis & Garrison, 1979).

Seasoned or experienced employees may not require as much attention; however, they need to know that if they ever need support, mentoring, attention, or extra help, they do have access to it.

Now, some employees simply may not feel comfortable in asking for help or support, even when it is available, which is why employers need to reassert their support constantly.

This can be accomplished either individually with each employee whenever possible, or during meetings. Reassertion encourages even shy employees to step forward and ask for support when they need it.

When employers get to know and understand their employees personally, they are at a greater advantage in gaining the respect, loyalty, and dedication of their employees.

4. Self-Pride and Satisfaction Needs

A classified employment ad in a European newspaper read "Wanted Surface Engineer... apply at ... Hotel..." The ad was peculiar enough to attract the curiosity of a Hotel Management professor at the Hotel Institute Montreux in Switzerland. The professor found the ad interesting since he was unfamiliar with the position advertised. So, he called the sponsoring hotel to enquire what a "Surface Engineer" was, what the duties entailed, and what qualifications were necessary.

Based on the title, it appeared to be a technical position that required some engineering degree. Surprisingly, the professor discovered that a "Surface Engineer" is a person who polishes marble flooring using a buffing machine, and no formal education is necessary for this position. It is an entry-level position as a part of the Engineering department maintenance crew. After further investigation, the professor learned that this particular hotel was aware of the importance of "Job Titles" to employees.

Employees need to be proud of what they do for a living; they need to be able to think and talk about their jobs with a sense of pride, importance, and accomplishment, regardless of where they may rank in an organization. In the example presented earlier, a hotel took the title of an entry-level position, which in most other companies would be labeled as "Floor Polisher" or in some cases even a "Janitor," and transformed it into a title that exudes glamour, sophistication, and importance. Furthermore, it added substantial weight and credibility to the job performed by the employee who will occupy the position.

Some organizations are still attached to the ancient mentality of keeping things the way they are, while wiser organizations have realized the psychological impact of titles on employees and the public at large. A slight manipulation of an employee's job title will reflect greatly the attractiveness of a position to prospective employees.

Employees with modified job titles are prouder of what they do and where they work. They tend to speak more positively and comfortably about their job, with an appreciation for the organization that has given them a title to be worthy of boasting about.

The following is a sample list of traditional titles within the hotel industry along with recommended alternatives:

Table 4. Traditional and Suggested Replacements

Traditional Titles	Suggested Titles
Bellboy / Porter / Bellhop/ Bellman	Luggage Coordinator
Busboy / Busgirl / Busser	Sanitation Agent
Receptionist / Front Desk Clerk / Front Desk Agent	Guest Services Agent

Emperor Napoleon Bonaparte understood the psychological impact that titles, uniforms, and visible displays of recognition had on both his soldiers (employees) as well as the greater public. He was credited with the establishment of the Legion of Honors, a military decoration, and with issuing thousands of crosses to be worn by his soldiers as recognition. He also bestowed the title of "Marshal of France" to many of his generals as a form of distinction for their achievements. Though he was criticized for creating seemingly grandiose titles and ribbons, Napoleon's techniques of giving titles and authority worked extremely well for him. It resulted in an army of loyal followers and countless battle victories (Carnegie, 1982).

Modifying job titles does not cost employers anything; it is one of the largest free job incentives an employer can offer. Surprisingly, not many companies utilize this incentive or realize its effect on employees.

Recognition

If it is true that employees get compensated for the job they do, then why do they expect their employers to acknowledge hard work, dedication, outstanding services, and/or great skills? Just as employers are ready to call employees on mistakes, tardiness, or poor performance, employers need to recognize an employee when they perform well. Recognition tells employees that all the extra effort they put into their work is noticed and appreciated. Employees take pride in recognition; it motivates them to continue performing at optimum levels and inspires them to attain further recognition by enhancing their abilities and service. Paul Keel, Former Vice President of Food and Beverage for the Hilton Hotels Corporation, supports this claim with this statement: "By getting them more recognition, we'll give them more pride, and that benefits all of us."

Employers often get so caught up in their daily work that they fail to recognize the sincere effort exerted by employees around them. Recognition comes in different forms such as: pay raises, day offs, duty exemptions, and notes of recognition. More often than not, employees yearn for a simple pat on the back or a verbal acknowledgment like: "thank you" or "well done." Recognition of employees is a form of appreciation, an expression that allows them to feel valued.

B.F. Skinner, a renowned psychologist, scientifically proved through his experiments that animals learned more rapidly and were able to retain what they learned more effectively when rewarded compared to animals that were punished for bad behavior. Later studies have proven the same applies to humans (Carnegie, 1982).

Duties

Job satisfaction comes from the knowledge that an employee's duties are recognized by one's superiors, and are of significance to their department, the company, and the industry. Employees need to feel a sense of fulfillment to experience job satisfaction. Addressing this issue is not an easy task for employers, yet it is not an impossible one. While some may feel that job satisfaction is a personal issue for employees to deal with, fulfillment is a mutual effort between employees and employers that helps in creating job satisfaction. Basically, employees and employers should look at each other and identify the things they need in one another.

Employees' responsibilities toward job satisfaction include:

1. Ensuring that they are aware of and comfortable with the duties involved in the jobs they are applying for.
2. Not applying for a position with a company if they have any reservations regarding the line of work, the pay, tasks, or even the reputation of the company.

Employers' responsibilities toward job satisfaction include:

1. Explaining all the responsibilities of a job to applicants, such as duties, hours, physical requirements (standing/sitting long hours), speed and accuracy involved in the job, company standards, and expectations.
2. Explaining the importance of each employee's position with regards to the whole organization and how that position contributes to the success of the organization.

No job in the hotel industry is insignificant. Each person is a key element to the success of an organization. If we were able to take a hotel Telephone Operator's position and analyze it in terms of rank, pay, duties, and contribution to the success of a hotel; we would learn how a Telephone Operator could make or break the reputation of a hotel. The following analysis of a Telephone Operator's position will demonstrate the previous statement:

Analysis of a Telephone/PBX Operator's Position

Rank: Entry-level position, low in terms of overall organizational structure.

Pay: Low hourly wage, in many cases close to minimum wage.

Duties: Respond to incoming calls. Transfer calls to appropriate destinations. Assist guests with inquiries. Receive wake-up call requests and carry them out. Dispatch guest requests and complaints to the appropriate personnel.

Contribution: They are the first impression for callers. A combination of their skills and performance directly affects the revenue of the hotel through failing or succeeding in gaining guest satisfaction.

A quick look at the duties of an operator may suggest to us that it is a low-skill job, which may or may not impact the profitability of a hotel greatly. However, nothing can be further from the truth. A closer examination of this position would demonstrate how critical a role an operator plays in the success and profitability of a hotel.

When a meeting planner contacts the hotel to enquire about reservations and booking banquet space, it is the operator who assists those potential event planners by directing them to the appropriate department. If they do not handle or transfer the call appropriately, it could mean the loss of thousands of dollars in potential revenue.

If the operators were not there to respond to in-house calls, guests would be furious. Their calls would be ignored; their requests and needs would not be met. As a result, guests would refuse to pay for their rooms. Some would depart the hotel and never return, and others with future reservations would cancel them and find other hotels with better service. On top of all that, negative publicity of poor service would spread through social media and word of mouth when upset guests tell their families, friends, and colleagues about the horrible experience they had with the hotel. All of this could happen if there was no telephone operator to answer the telephone.

Similarly, if all the Dishwashers or Stewards quit or do not show up to work, a hotel restaurant, banquet facility, or room services cannot operate. You cannot serve food if you don't have clean dishes. It's as simple as that!

One of the lowest-paying jobs within a Food & Beverage department can cripple the operation and impact revenue. Think about that for a moment and let that sink in.

Each employee needs to know how significant their positions are within the realm of the organization they are in. That knowledge contributes to an employee's self-worth and, consequently, self-pride.

5. Self-Actualization Needs

At the top of the Hierarchy of Needs is the need for Self-Actualization, a societal need certain people possess. This is a need that inspires people to fulfill deeds that go beyond simply benefiting themselves. This inspiration and selfless dedication created people such as Gandhi, Nelson Mandela, and Mother Teresa, all of whom dedicated their whole lives to worthy causes they believed in.

In the hotel industry, many talented and dedicated individuals are committed to helping their organizations and industry grow. Experienced and passionate employees often seek to develop their colleagues and work environment while expanding their skills. These individuals are always there to assist others by lending a helping hand, assisting in training new employees, and volunteering their services to develop their departments and organizations. In a sense, these are the pioneers and visionaries of the industry, leading the way to a brighter and more advanced future.

Although many talented and dedicated individuals work in the hotel industry, not everyone is committed to developing themselves, their industry, or others. For those who are committed, their efforts must be recognized and appreciated.

Employers can assist employees in fulfilling this need for Self-Actualization by providing a forum for employees to present, discuss, and initiate their ideas and contributions. A common historical practice by many organizations was to place suggestion boxes or a departmental idea board where employees can submit their suggestions. Today, some companies also provide a virtual online suggestion box.

The best suggestions are sometimes selected and implemented. To encourage this practice, some employers offer incentives or rewards for good ideas. In 1993, baristas at a California Starbucks saw an opportunity to add a new product that would be popular in the summer season and increase sales. They began experimenting with flavored blended coffee drinks and developed what eventually became one of the most profitable beverages on Starbucks' menu, the Frappuccino (Schultz, 2012).

Unfortunately, suggestion boxes and idea boards are often failures. This is primarily because employers fail to set these programs up for success by not having a plan of action for the ideas received. Nor have they developed a process that transforms the suggestions from words to an operable reality.

Some employers frequently rob employees of the right to claim any credit for suggestions that are chosen. Some employers even advertise the fact that they are stealing employees' ideas by going as far as placing statements on suggestion boxes or idea boards that state, "All ideas once submitted and accepted are property of the company."

Furthermore, employees making suggestions that are selected by the company are not included in the planning and implementation of their idea. By engaging in this demeaning and unethical practice, some employers indirectly communicate that they value good ideas from employees, but do not believe that employees are smart enough or capable enough to implement their own ideas.

To ensure the cultivation and fulfillment of Self-Actualization Needs employers need to allow their employees to be able to express their thoughts and apply their suggestions, or at least to test them out, to confirm whether they would work.

Employers also need to provide employees with the necessary resources to implement their suggestions.

The Ritz-Carlton Hotel chain gives employees the right to be involved in the planning of the work that affects them.

"To create pride and joy in the workplace, all employees have the right to be involved in the planning of the work that affects them." - (The Ritz-Carlton Hotel Company, 1998).

This is a written statement that all leaders working for the Ritz-Carlton are required to respect and abide by. The Ritz-Carlton is a company that truly believes that line employees are experts in their own area and are the ones that can contribute significantly to its development.

Chapter Five:
Seeking Answers

"Curiosity is the very basis of education and if you tell me that curiosity killed the cat, I say only the cat died nobly."
- Arnold Edinborough

Years ago, when I originally embarked on a journey to discover some of the causes that led to voluntary turnover, I decided to approach my work from a quantitative perspective; however, at the time, the availability of literature on the topic and datasets were sparse and inaccessible. My burning curiosity about the subject matter and a handful of recent publications dealing with employee turnover and employee retention provided the platform from which I launched my study.

In order to acquire data that represents different perspectives within the hotel industry, I developed three surveys to gain background knowledge of the survey participants, as well as possible reasons for voluntary employee turnover.

The surveys included various types of questions, such as open-ended, closed-ended, multiple-choice, and scaled questions. I used open-ended questions to allow respondents to freely express their opinions. These responses would help generate ideas that could uncover overlooked factors. The open-ended questions also aimed to elicit responses that could be used by employers in the hotel industry to improve employee retention.

Hotels come in a variety of sizes, styles, service levels, focus, locations, and target guests. So, I wanted to ensure that I had a broad representation of the responses that I received. The participants that I contacted for my survey included employees from various departments, position levels, and hotel brands throughout the San Gabriel Valley in Los Angeles County. This included bell staff, front desk staff, PBX operators, directors of food & beverage, banquet managers, restaurant and banquet servers, rooms executives, human resources managers, engineers, general managers, and other positions. Thirty participants were contacted, and the response rate was 70%.

The data I collected through this survey by no means represents definitive quantitative information upon which uncontested conclusions may be drawn. This is due to the following reasons: firstly, the survey sample is restricted to a minute group of participants, therefore it is not large enough to represent the entire industry. Secondly, the scope of my research was limited geographically. However, the data collected represents valuable qualitative feedback directly from the individuals involved with the hotel industry in some capacity.

These individuals have either experienced or had to work with voluntary turnover in the hotel industry. The interviewees' experiences in the hotel industry ranged from 3 to 18 years, so they all had sufficient experience to provide answers to my questions.

Chapter Six:
Answers

At the beginning of my journey of discovery, I had hoped to uncover the factors that lead so many hoteliers to voluntarily quit. In doing so, I aimed to answer several questions that would help me better understand why people join the hotel industry, why some of them stay while others quit, which departments have the highest turnover rates, and what solutions human resources departments and hoteliers may offer to address this problem. Here's what I discovered through the verbatim responses that I received from survey participants and interviewees:

1. Why do people join the Hotel Industry?

The hotel industry is an exciting and diverse field that offers a continually challenging work environment. Many joined the hotel industry because they loved meeting new and different people daily, as well as the challenges and opportunities presented with that diversity. Some employees were simply inclined towards customer interactions, and hotels provide the type of environment they wanted to be in.

Some joined the hotel industry because it was their major in college, and they enjoyed the work and human interaction. Among management employees surveyed or interviewed, 56% held a degree in Hotel Management or Business Administration, and some held degrees in both. The other 44% of the respondents held degrees not related to the hotel industry in any way. These degrees included majors such as history, sociology, liberal arts, philosophy, geography, and administration of justice.

Others, including myself, were recommended by friends who were hoteliers. Others joined because it gave them flexible work hours to do other things or as a part-time second job.

When analyzing the data, a couple of revelations became immediately apparent to me. Nearly all the responses had to do with needs 2 through 5 on the Hierarchy of Employee Needs *(Job Security & Stability Needs, Self-Pride and Satisfaction, Emotional Needs, and Self-Actualization)*. It was as though the first and most basic need on the hierarchy, *Physical Work Environment Needs*, was assumed to be present by these participants before they joined.

2. Why do some people stay, while others quit?

Many employees stated that they stayed in the hotel industry because they loved their job and enjoyed working with guests. They also stayed because of the availability of opportunities in their field of expertise and the excellent advancement opportunities offered by the industry. The hotel industry is global, and as a hotelier, you can work anywhere, explore different positions, and rise through the ranks rapidly if you wish and are willing to relocate.

Some intended to make a career in this industry because they loved it and never experienced the same day twice. Others stayed because they possessed diverse backgrounds and adaptability. Some had the family support needed to allow them to pursue their professional aspiration, which included relocating if necessary to succeed. In short, the hotel industry offered a unique combination of people, business, and opportunities that kept employees engaged and motivated.

3. What hotel departments experience the highest turnover rates?

The data in this section was provided by the human resources managers I surveyed. The responses were very consistent. The following table presents a cumulative ranking of departmental turnover, starting with the department that has the highest turnover to the lowest:

Table 5. Cumulative Departmental Ranking for Turnover

Ranking	Department
1	Housekeeping *(Highest turnover)*
2	Front Office
3	Engineering
4	Food & Beverage
5	Sales & Marketing
	Security/Loss Prevention
6	Human Resources Accounting
7	General Management
	Purchasing *(Lowest turnover)*

Having worked in every department within the industry, I was not surprised by this data. Housekeeping is a physically demanding and low-paying job, with little reward or recognition, and in many companies, it fails to meet most of the needs on the Hierarchy of Employee Needs such as *Physical Work Environment, Job Security & Stability Needs, and Self-Pride and Satisfaction.*

4. What are the top 10 reasons hotel employees quit?

Participants were given a set of possible reasons to select from. These reasons were then categorized as either cause or effect and mapped to the appropriate hierarchical employee need as shown in Table 6.

Table 6. Survey Options and Classifications

Reasons for voluntary terminations	Cause/ Effect	Need Classification
Career change	Effect	Self-Actualization
Commute	Cause	Physical Work Environment
Corporate culture	Cause	Emotional
Did not get along with my boss	Cause	Emotional
Family reasons	Cause	Job Security & Stability
Found better employment opportunity	Effect	Job Security & Stability
Lack of advancement opportunities	Cause	Job Security & Stability
Lack of communication	Cause	Job Security & Stability
Lack of job satisfaction	Cause	Self-Pride and Satisfaction
Lack of recognition	Cause	Self-Pride and Satisfaction
Low pay / benefits	Cause	Job Security & Stability
Relocating	Effect	Job Security & Stability
Retiring	Effect	Self-Actualization
Stress	Cause	Physical Work Environment
Training	Cause	Physical Work Environment
Working hours	Cause	Physical Work Environment

The data was then filtered to focus on the most selected reason that was designated as a cause, rather than effect. When comparing the results from the surveys, a distinct pattern emerged. The number one reason for voluntary terminations in all surveys was "Found better employment", which is an effect rather than a cause.

Most employees believed that another employer had something better to offer them. This raises the question, "What is it that other employers have to offer that is currently either not provided or not sufficiently provided to maintain employee loyalty?"

The answer to this question lies in the other reasons selected by the respondents for voluntary turnover, which were classified as causes. When analyzing the results of each survey on an inferential level, it is obvious that each selected factor for voluntary terminations is a result of another. The reason "Found better employment" is a product of other factors. Figure 1 presents the combined results of all the Former Employee, Head of Department, and Human Resources surveys. The combined results display the frequency of selected factors leading to voluntary terminations along with the percentage of the responses.

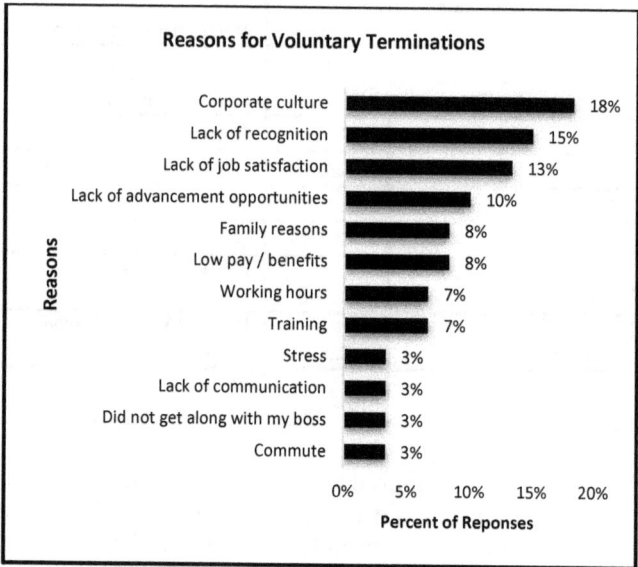

Reasons for Voluntary Terminations

Reasons	Percent of Reponses
Corporate culture	18%
Lack of recognition	15%
Lack of job satisfaction	13%
Lack of advancement opportunities	10%
Family reasons	8%
Low pay / benefits	8%
Working hours	7%
Training	7%
Stress	3%
Lack of communication	3%
Did not get along with my boss	3%
Commute	3%

Figure 1. Survey Results Reasons for Voluntary Termination

The results of the survey are consistent with the observations made by Ashby and Pell (2001) in their book *Embracing Excellence*, when they stated that " ...the real reasons for discontent lie deep in the culture of the organization." It is often said that people may not remember you as a boss, as a coach, as a trainer, as a supervisor, or as a colleague for the things that you necessarily did or accomplished, but they will remember you for the way you made them feel.

The emotional needs of employees emerged in this survey as the most crucial requirement. Employees may be willing to work for less money provided their core emotional needs are met by their employers and their values align with those of the companies they work for.

5. What solutions do human resources departments propose to reduce voluntary employee turnover?

In attempting to find solutions for the voluntary turnover in the hotel industry, we simply asked hoteliers, including human resource managers, what they would do differently if they could make changes. Responses to this question greatly varied; however, there were similar ideas that could be grouped.

One group suggested:

- establishing a professional, well-administered, and structured training program
- increasing wages and establishing incentive programs
- introducing empowerment
- terminating toxic managers who compromise the mission and the corporate culture with more competent ones

Another group suggested that open-door policies to allow employees to feel that their managers were accessible and open to hearing their ideas, concerns, and feedback could help reduce employee turnover. It would make employees feel that they were important, and mattered as individuals and professionals.

Finally, the third group suggested ensuring that leaders who were hired were aligned with the company's objectives. This would ensure that those leaders understood, subscribed, and actively worked towards a company's mission and philosophy.

It is not surprising that the solutions to addressing the high turnover rate in the industry seem like common sense business practices that are well articulated by those already within the industry.

Chapter Seven:
Conclusion

Although I had a notion as to why hotel employees voluntarily quit their jobs, I was surprised at the repetitiveness of some of the responses in the survey and the direction they led. My preconceived notions and the results of the study have all confirmed that the voluntary turnover problem can often be traced back to management.

As unfortunate as the hotel industry is with the overwhelming turnover rate that plagues it, there is a silver lining to this problem. The high turnover rate that currently exists provides managers and employers with a greater pool of feedback from employees who voluntarily resign. This allows employers to explore the reasons that lead to voluntary turnover at their company more easily. Employers as such are presented with the gift to unravel the mysteries that contribute to their human resources problem and act upon it to increase employee retention.

Through discussions with several professionals in the hotel industry, I have realized that many leaders and human resources executives are under the misconception that "burn-out" is a leading cause of many voluntary turnovers. Although "burn-out" may be the most apparent reason, employers and managers need to understand that "burn-out" is merely the result of other factors. It is an effect, not the cause of voluntary turnover.

My research suggests that "Corporate Culture" is a leading cause of voluntary turnover in the industry. This conclusion is consistent with industry research and publications. If I were to define corporate culture, it would go something like this:

"Corporate Culture is the values, behaviors, and traits that are instilled and exercised within an organization. Corporate culture stems from the visions of the founders, is guided by the mission of the organization, driven by organizational leaders, and enriched by employees."

Many organizations excel at envisioning and setting idealistic missions, yet they often fail in instilling the behaviors they aspire to achieve. Since behaviors and traits can be learned, employers and managers desperately need to have well-developed plans for structured recruitment, training, recognition, employee development, and succession planning, which deliver the measurable results targeted.

So where should companies begin?

I would say that they need to begin with an intention!

In other words, companies need to set a goal to commit to genuinely working towards addressing this issue and dedicating time and resources to it. The problem will not fix itself! It will not happen without intentionality, purpose, energy, honesty, investment, and some growing pains.

They would then need to conduct an open and authentic analysis of a company's culture, policies, and practices, as well as an employee climate survey to determine how the company is doing to meet their employee's needs and expectations. Companies also need to assess whether their practices align with the company's mission and vision.

There isn't a solution that will eliminate voluntary turnover, but the least companies can do is focus on mitigating the problem and stop hemorrhaging good employees due to corporate culture, poor management practices, and a lack of competent, ethical, and transformational leadership.

People often seek answers to their problems in a distant place beyond their walls and often among strangers when all they really ought to do is look within.

About the Author

Dr. Fawaz Al-Malood is a former hotelier turned educator. Dr. Al-Malood received his academic and professional training in Hospitality Management, Business Administration, and Education Management in Bahrain, the United Arab Emirates, Switzerland, the United States, and South Africa. Prior to joining academia, Dr. Al-Malood held positions with companies like The Ritz-Carlton, Hilton, Starwood, and other corporate organizations.

Dr. Al-Malood was a tenured professor of hospitality management for 12 years. He also several leadership positions within academia including program director, department chair, and associate dean, CFO, and Trustee.

He is currently a college administrator, author, YouTuber, blogger, and podcaster. He is the Founder of FacultyWorkshop.com, a blog dedicated to sharing successful strategies for teaching, productivity, and professional development for college educators.

Dr. Al-Malood holds a doctorate in Education Management from the University of South Africa, an MBA, and an MS in Management and Leadership from Western Governors University, a bachelor in Hotel, Restaurant, and Tourism Administration from the University of South Carolina, and a Diploma in Hotel Management from the prestigious Hotel Institute Montreux in Switzerland.

References

Ashby, F. C., & Pell, A. R. (2001). *Embracing Excellence: Become An Employer Of Choice To Attract And Keep The Best Talent.* Prentice Hall Press.

Belilos, C. (1999). *Conducting Effective Employee Orientations.* http://www.hotel-online.com/Neo/News/PressReleases1999_1st/

Carey, K. (2002). *Color Psychology and Affect on Business.* Small Talk Marketing & Communications, Inc. http://www.kirst-incarey.com/Pages/FreeArticlesColorPink.htm

Carnegie, D. (1982). *How to Win Friends And Influence People.* Pocket Books.

Chetri, R. (2021). *Turnover Intention and Motivation: Quantitative Correlational Examination of a Federal Agency.* https://www.proquest.com/docview/2623031603?pq-origsite=gscholar&fromopenview=true

Davis, R. L., & Garrison, P. A. (1979). *Mentoring: In Search Of a Taxonomy* [(Masters Thesis).]. Massachusetts Institute of Technology.

Handelsman, J. (1998). *Understanding and Remedying Employee Turnover.* http://www.toolkit.cch.com/columns/people/138turnover.asp

Kennedy, D. J., & Berger, F. (1994). Newcomer Socialization: Oriented to Facts or Feelings? *Cornell Hotel and Restaurant Administration Quarterly, 35*(6),

58–71.
https://doi.org/10.1177/001088049403500613

Levin, M. (2018). *Harvard Research Proves Toxic Employees Destroy Your Culture and Your Bottom Line*. Inc.Com. https://www.inc.com/marissa-levin/harvard-research-proves-toxic-employees-destroy-your-culture-your-bottom-line.html

Payne, K. D. (1998). *Employee Turnover: It's Keeping Me From Having a Boat!* http://www.hotel-online.com/Neo/Trends/Payne/Articles/ Employee_Turnover.htm

Peters, T. (2002). Boss Talk: Top CEOs Share the Ideas That Drive the World's Most Successful Companies. *By The Editors Of The Wall Street Journal.*

Schultz, H. (2012). *Pour Your Heart Into It: How Starbucks Built a Company One Cup at a Time.* Hachette Books.

Shanahan, T. (2000). *Recruit and Hire Differently, Reduce Turnover, and Save Lots of Money.* http://www.hotel-online.com/Neo/News/

Smith, G. (2001). *Here Today, Here Tomorrow: Transforming Your Workforce from High-Turnover to High-Retention.* Dearborn Trade Publishing.

Stutts, A. (2001). *Retaining Human Capital Through Assessment.* http://www.hotel-online.com/Neo/News/PR2001_4th/Oct01_/

The Ritz-Carlton Hotel Company. (1998). *The Ritz-Carlton Basics.* The Ritz-Carlton Basics Credo Card.

Woods, R. (2012). *Managing Hospitality Human Resources* (5th ed.). Educational Institute of the American Hotel and Motel Association.

www.ingramcontent.com/pod-product-compliance
Lightning Source LLC
Chambersburg PA
CBHW070947280326
41934CB00009B/2029